Sunsets and Soul Care

All photos in this book were taken by the author, without filters or modification, without professional training. We invite you to do the same.

ISBN 978-1-7330674-9-2

A ministry resource from

Published by

PO Box 3619
Vista, CA 92085

Scripture verses are quoted from the HOLY BIBLE, NEW INTERNATIONAL VERSION ®
Copyright © 1973, 1978, 1984 by International Bible Society. Used by permission of Zondervan.
All rights reserved.

Also quoted: Frank Laubach, Learning the Vocabulary of God:
A Spiritual Diary (Nashville: Upper Room, 1956), p.9. Public Domain.

All other written content is the original work of the author.

Sunsets
and
Soul Care

ARLANA SCOLA, ThM

WILSON ALEX
HOLLAND

JANUARY 22, 1932 - DECEMBER 3, 2015

To a Life Well Lived

DEDICATION

I dedicate this devotional to my father, Wilson Alex Holland, who taught me many things. One of which is the love of photography.

I hope that you find peace, joy, comfort, and care for your soul within these pages.

May you be blessed with peaceful nights and gentle days,

Arlana

Welcome to a peace-filled journey, with the goal of caring for your soul.

Breathe deep, begin the journey with me of peace and soul care.

Immerse yourself in each of these sunsets. Notice the nuances of light and shadow. See how each one is unique, never to be repeated. Realize that each sunset's beauty is a once-in-a-lifetime event!

Remember to pause because... when we pause we can better understand our "because."

Pause Because

Pause because... taking time for yourself is a priceless gift that provides endless benefits.

Pause because... the ministry of presence to yourself and to your soul is important.

Pause because... You love your family.

Pause because... You are exhausted.

Pause because... You are thankful.

Pause because... The sunset is beautiful.

Pause because... Soul care is absolutely necessary.

Pause because............................?

Between sunsets in this devotional, you will find several pages like this. Pages that invite you to turn your gaze inward, to breathe, and to listen to your own soul; to pause.

Our souls are the inner wellspring of God's grace. God's grace to us and *through* us!

Attending to the inner promptings of your soul takes practice, but is always worth doing.

You will find rest for your soul.

- Matthew 11:29

Learn the unforced rhythms of grace. The rest that Jesus promises is love, healing, and peace within your soul. Sit back and enjoy caring for your soul.

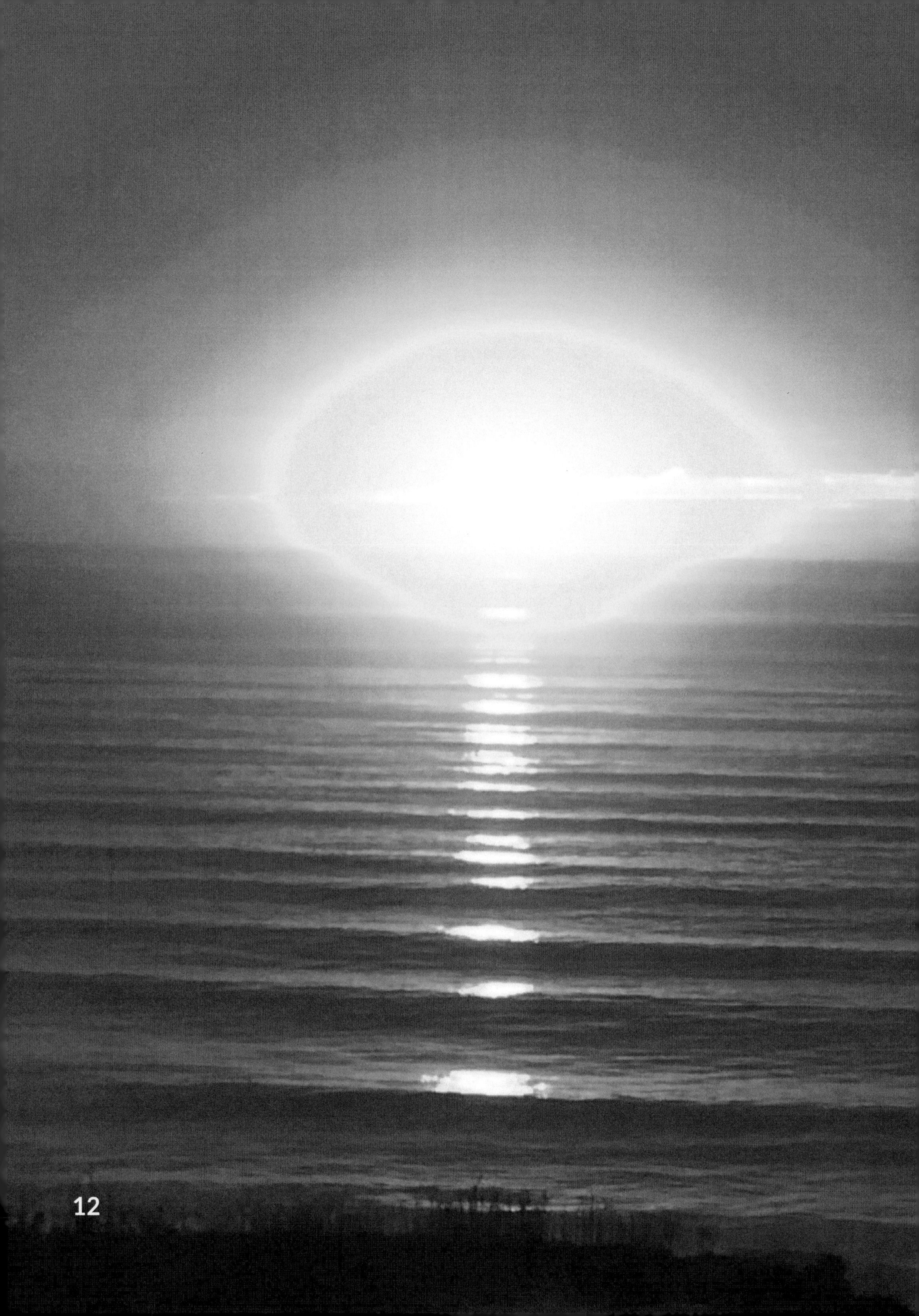

Embrace the tranquility that is deeply embedded in your soul. Take a breath and experience this peace as you bask in the glory of a sunset.

19

Moments of stillness are full of promise, power, and purpose. Time spent being still is never wasted. It is an investment in your personal soul care.

Peace I leave with you,
My peace I give to you.

- John 14:27

24

Peacefulness is a priceless state of mind. Within the depths of our peace we find the hands of God and care for our souls.

He restores my soul.

- Psalm 23:3

Be present to the glory in a sunset, let your soul be restored.

Breathe. Take in the color, the light, and the shadow. Number the different colors as you number your blessings.

The Lord will not take you along paths that are not designed specifically for you. It may not make sense in the moment. Patiently enjoy the glory of the sunset and await understanding.

The joy of the Lord is my strength.

- Nehemiah 8:10

Take a moment to ponder the beauty provided each day as a gift given just to you. Just as we delight in the beauty and glory of His creation, He delights in us.

Do everything in love.

- 1st Corinthians 16:14

Love is as powerful and as beautiful as a sunset. Love sets the stage for beautiful things to happen. When you allow it to, a sunset can set the stage for kind, loving, and compassionate thoughts. Use a moment with a sunset to ignite the love in your heart and soul and give it as a gift to someone.

Seek peace and pursue it.

- Psalm 34:14

Peace is a gift that is as powerful as love. Find peace as you experience a sunset and share that peace with others.

49

Behold, you are beautiful.

- Song of Solomon 1:4

The beauty of your soul is illuminated in the glow of a sunset.

The rhythm of the seasons, the rhythm of our bodies, the rhythm of the sunset... they all reflect beauty in our surroundings and in our soul.

She is more precious than rubies.

- Proverbs 3:15

Yes she is!

61

See the beauty in ALL things as you witness the beauty in a sunset.

He has made everything beautiful in its time.

- Ecclesiastes 3:11

Things may appear different to us than they did in the past.

As with the sun, a new day with new opportunity will always begin its movement into our presence.

Act justly, love mercy, walk humbly.

- Micah 6:8

- From *Sunshine in My Soul* by Elisa E. Hewitt, 1887

Whatever you do, work at it with all your heart.

- Colossians 3:23

73

As you are present with a sunset, listen to a piece of music that moves you. Sing to the sunset as it sings to your soul.

With God all things are possible.

- Matthew 19:26

Every single sunset has been different, never duplicated since the beginning of time.

How amazing!

In times of turbulence and the unknown, one sunset can bring calm to the soul. It reiterates that God's creativity and beauty are always at work.

The Lord will guide you always.

- Isaiah 58:11

81

I will praise you, oh Lord, with all my heart.

- Psalm 9:1

Wisdom and discernment abound within stillness,
and when you "show up" for an encounter with God.

The Lord will fight for you,
you need only to be still.

- Exodus 14:14

Try putting all the noise aside, pause and be still. The answers to your questions will arrive when you least expect them.

Deep within us all there is an amazing inner sanctuary of the soul, a holy place, a divine center, a speaking voice, to which we may continuously return.

- Thomas Kelly, 1893-1941

My soul finds rest in God alone.

- Psalm 62:1

"God, what is man's best gift to mankind?"

"To be of beautiful soul, then to let people see into your soul."

- Frank Laubach

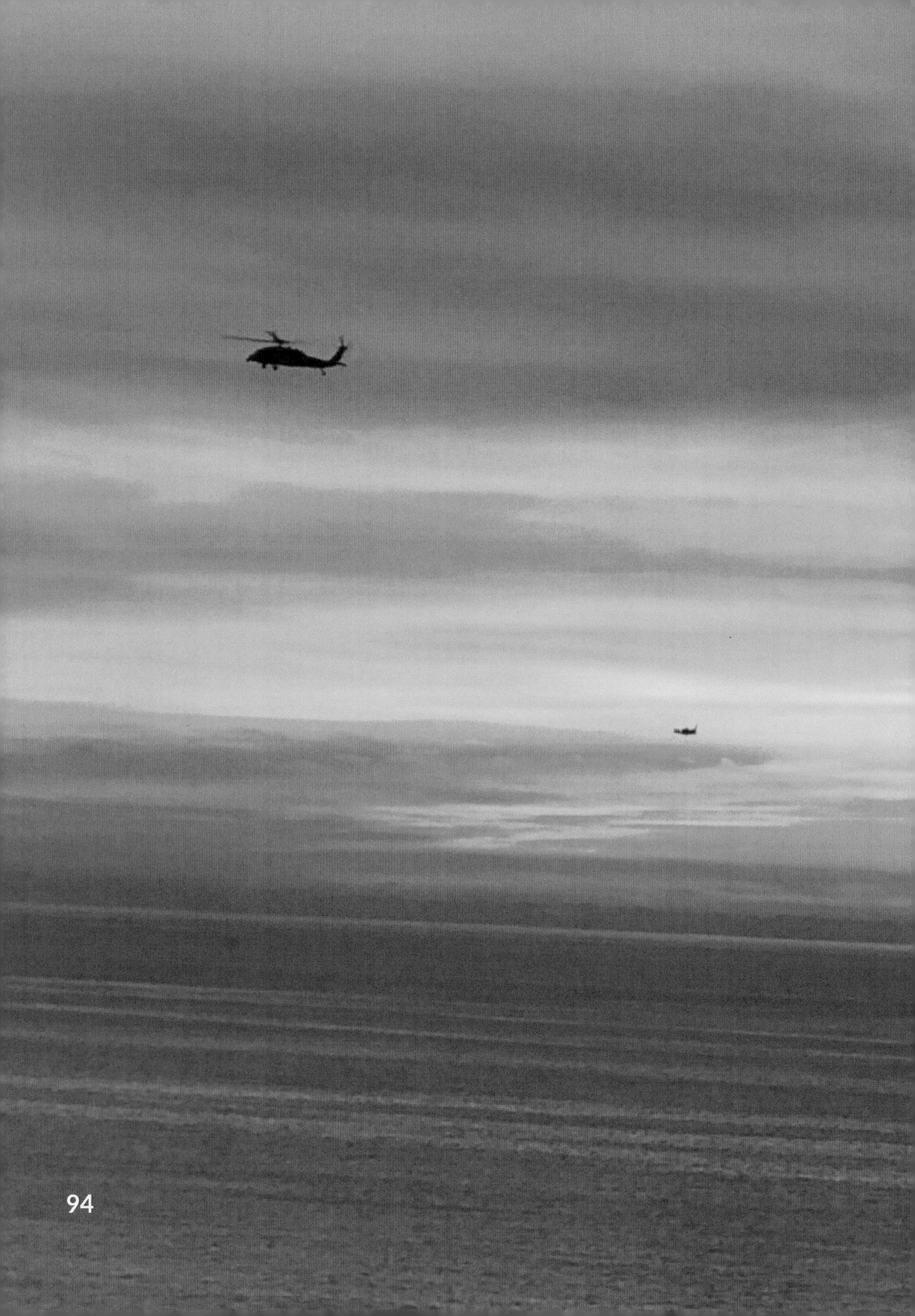

Soul care is an endless pursuit that provides endless benefits to self and others.

97

Let there be light.

- Gen 1:3

When day was distinguished from night
the beauty of sunset was created.

Be thankful for every sunset you have the joy to witness.

Some are breathtaking, vibrant with color, shadow, and nuance. Others pass with little distinction or fanfare. Each is beautiful in its own way.

Be thankful for the invitation each sunset offers to pause and enjoy, to restore your soul.

YOUR TURN!

For a complimentary 2-page guide to nurturing your own habit of soul-care, visit: www.TheRubyRedSlippers.com/guides

You'll also find links to podcasts, our mailing list, and social media resources.

Did this book help you in some way? Did it miss the mark? Please tell us about it! If you'd be so kind, post a review for this book on Amazon mentioning what stood out to you. Readers trust other readers most, which is exactly how things should be.

COMING SOON:

Devotional for Grief

The Ruby Red Slippers Way

A Ruby Red Slippers Anthology

ABOUT THE AUTHOR

Ariana is an experienced and talented encourager. She uses her deep understanding of God's word to encourage others in their spiritual journey and provides spiritual direction.

Her experience includes: pastor of CARE ministry, women's retreat leader, keynote speaker, hospice chaplaincy, plus chaplaincy both in prison ministry and juvenile hall. Whether on horseback, leading a large group, or one-on-one, God's words of encouragement are always present.

Ariana has a Masters in Theology from Bethel Theological Seminary. Her family has grown into two adult sons, their wives, and one grandson. She and her husband live in San Diego, CA. She loves the Lord, horseback riding, photography, nature, and helping others. She is the founder of The Ruby Red Slippers Foundation.

Made in the USA
Monee, IL
05 April 2022

89f8adc2-e090-4c50-b7df-d7b91ab68a87R01